Closer to the Sun

Screenplay from the film project by Nick Peterson

I0117945

DiaryUnlimited.com

Closer to the Sun was originally published in 2011 by The Edge Press (UK) and DiaryUnlimited (U.S.)

Published as a DiaryUnlimited.com paperback by The Edge Press. AnotherClip.com

Printed in the USA

ISBN 978-0-9822924-2-6

www.DiaryUnlimited.com

Design and Layout by Tom Norwood

Contents

Closer to the Sun
By Nick Peterson

Short Summary

Four investigators are assembled by an insurance company in New York to examine a claim for accidental death of six oil workers on an oil platform, off the coast of Nigeria.

Synopsis

The team has 24 hours to investigate the claim. It slowly transpires that it wasn't accidental death but that the oil workers have been taken hostage by local terrorists, a common occurrence that often goes without victims and in this case six men had died.

How to approve the claim when there are so many overwhelming evidences against it? The trouble is for a reputable international insurance company dismissing such a claim would place them at odds with the real problems in the country, place them on the spot as an unlikely human right witness and will compromise a whole system with ramifications to powerful Western governments and multinational companies. They have accidentally walked into highly dangerous grounds and the only way forward is to honour the claim. The investigators are not happy about the final outcome, but a decision is being made to honour the claim.

Notes and Development

The action revolves inside a room "The White Room" where four investigators are seated around a table and are examining stacks of documents.

The other characters, the crew inside the oil rig Delta 12 are seen through a series of pictures shuffled around the table by the inspectors and during "The Massacre" (Scene 13). The logs filed by members of the crew of the oil rig are read aloud by the investigators.

Some of the most intense scenes such as "The Massacre" described by DC inside the "Comm's room" is a live recording from DC's voice. The noise and the soundtrack are heard over; the screams, the sound of rifles and gun shots; all the terror taking place during that moment. The element of fear is felt and conveyed throughout the soundtrack and the reading of the log. This log is a 'real time' transcript of the audio recording made by DC that enhances the impression of being "live".

The report made by NP, the surviving member of the crew, when he is investigated by the military explains exactly what occurred and took place during "The Massacre".

The shrieking sound made by the seagulls, the storming sea, the gun shots, the screaming of both the pirates and the crew members; everything can be heard in the background.

The main film footage is created from inside the "White Room". It is where the action takes place.

When a picture is grabbed by one of the investigators, the image or document is then zoomed in and panned slowly over.

All files, documents, maps and pictures of the oil rig are presented in this way but more slowly than in a documentary with the corresponding background noise and music.

The "Massacre" scene is presented like a painting; panning from left to right very slowly for one minute focusing on all the details of the scene thus enhancing the power of its content. Only the music, some background noise and the beginning of the voice over for the log can be heard. The image displaced as a painting is then made even more alive by displaying the real footage of the scene with fresh blood still dripping down from some of the bodies. In the background the sound of the waves storming in the sea and the shrieking seagulls out of control are gradually amplified. The footage of the massive flock of insane seagulls is superimposed over the "live footage" of the scene (not the actual picture of it) with 'fade into' in between the image and the main footage of the scene. One of the investigators is reading the report made by the surviving crew member over the rest of the footage.

Climax
The climaxes of the film are the discovery of the
"Massacre" on the main Decks ("The Massacre", Scene 13),
the description of DC's log from the "Comm's room",
("The Situation" Scene 14) with the report of NP, one of the
only two survivors who went through "The Massacre".
"The Claim": the debate between the four investigators
when they are analyzing the claim ("The Claim" Scene 15).

Life on the Oil Platform
There are nine fit men between the age of 18 and 50
working on board of 'Delta 12' the oil platform. The men
are drawn from various countries, including the U.S,
France, Canada and the UK. They all live side by side.
They are all ex-military men.

The living quarters consist of a recreation room with TV
sets, tables and sofas, a large canteen, a kitchen, a gym and
the dorms: a large room with bunk beds.

There is very little heat and it's very cold, especially at
night. The living conditions are extremely harsh, the food
is lousy, the washrooms and the toilets although cleaned
up every day, are constantly filthy, dirty water is always
leaking over the floors.

There are no women on board. There is a captain and his
eight soldiers, all heavily armed with hand-guns and rifles,
always on duty. Everyone is the captain and the soldier.
There is a staff rotation in shifts.

There is no escape possible for the duration of the contract, which generally lasts a year. A worker may only leave on serious medical grounds or if dead. Death and suicides are a common occurrence.

Although thoroughly searched on arrival the oil workers often carry their own gun or knife, smuggled in once a month when the supply of food and goods is being delivered.

No cigarettes or drugs are allowed on the platform. Anyone found to contravene the rules will be confined to a cell with no light and no window for twenty-four or forty-eight hours depending on the crime.

A medical doctor comes in every three months to inspect the men and distribute medicines. No one would ever admit to any serious illness or disease as this would be interpreted as a sign of weakness. Any admission of weakness to fellow workers will drive anyone to suicide.

Every now and then a man escapes by plunging into the sea. No one has ever survived an escape as the sea is infested with sharks.

Mutiny is rare and when there is one the captain can order one of his soldiers to shoot or if it gets really serious the captain can send a message to the Nigerian coast guards and the army generally arrives in a jiffy.

Sometimes, an army ship, Nigerian or American is seen on the horizon.

The sea is always stormy but during the day the sun is always enormous and shines with an extremely powerful heat.

The work is extremely demanding, channelling the dig of oil for eight hours, one hour for lunch and some occasional breaks. The workers start their day at 5 am and the curfew, when all lights are switched off, at 10 pm.

Every week an oil cargo arrives to take a load of oil. Sometimes there is an attack from some sea pirates. They board the oil platform; take members of the crew hostage often with accomplices amongst the crew. Sometimes the pirates escape with their load of oil but most of the time the army is called in and it's when the carnage starts. It always leads to the death of some of the hostages.

The pirates who are captured are taken to the main land and are always hanged in Nigeria without trial.

This is the life on an oil platform off the coast of Africa, one of the most violent places on earth.

In spite of all this, there will always be someone willing to join a crew of the men on the many oil platforms.

Each man is reporting on everyone's daily life; each and one of them reports on everyone. It is a constant surveillance.

Each and one of them are the head and the keeper of the other. Everyone is watching one another. Everyone must keep a log of the events that will be emailed to The Sun's central office (their employer in Austin Texas, USA). Everyone is in charge or everyone believes it is so.

Characters
On the oil rig (main cast)
AP: Allan Patterson. U.S. ex-army
DC: Don Carradine. U.S. ex-army
DNC: Dabiel N. Caldley. U.S. ex-army
NP: Nathan Pearl. U.S. ex-marine
TN: Tom Nelson. Canadian, ex-army
GN: Geoff Nobst. U.S. ex-army
PR: Philippe Rowland, U.S. ex-marine
AE: AL Ellys. U.S. ex-army
ET: Etienne Dutoit, French. Ex-army

Characters description
AP: Allan Patterson. U.S. ex-army
26, male
Hair: Black
Weight: 12 St/ 82 Kg
Height: 6ft 4

Race: Caucasian
Specific signs: tattooed
He contracted a heroin addiction whilst at sea. When the
dependence is too severe the doctor in charge always
prescribes some pills of some kind to ease the need and
release the tension. In the U.S. army the use of heavy drugs
is a very sensitive and controversial subject. Officially,
there is none but when at war and programmed to kill,
there is little less that can help.

A job at sea on an oil rig is one of the only jobs available
for an ex-soldier leaving the army where he doesn't have
to fight or kill. In order to sustain the hardship endured at
sea there is nothing else to relieve the pressure. Smoking is
not allowed anywhere on the platform. Heroin is widely
available albeit in moderation. Officially there is none but
it is smuggled with the food.

No one knows where it's coming from or would admit it
being there, but it's there and it does the job.

Unofficially the company doesn't provide any needles. It is
however possible to inject heroin inside the infirmary. The
needles are often dumped at sea. There are long periods of
2-3 weeks without heroin and it's when the tension mounts
and fights occur amongst the crew.

Pills of some kind are provided as a substitute by the
medical officer in charge. Officially nothing is being
distributed.

No one really knows what the tablets contain. It tastes and feels like aspirin but works a treat. It seriously brings the tension down.

DC: Don Carradine. U.S. ex-army
22, male
Hair: Brown
Weight: 11 St / 75 Kg
Height: 5.11
Race: Caucasian
Specific signs: tattooed
No schooling known. It is believed that he was enrolled into the army in 2003. He worked for six months on an oil rig prior to Delta 12. It was his first oil job.
He was further distinguished by a perpetual blinking of the eyes, and this, together with the red tint of his complexion and a way he had of hanging his head forward and rolling it from side to side as he walked, gave him the appearance of an orangutan.

DNC: Dabiel N. Caldley. U.S. ex-army
38, male
Hair: Cropped/Grey
Weight: 12 St / 82 Kg
Height: 5ft 8"
Race: Caucasian

Specific signs: tattooed
A high school drop-out. He joined the army soon after. He went to war in Afghanistan in 2001-2003.

NP: Nathan Pearl. U.S. ex-marine
44, male
Hair: Red
Weight: 11 St / 75 Kg
Height: 6ft
Race: Caucasian
Specific signs: tattooed
A high school drop-out. He Joined the army soon after. He went to the war in Afghanistan in 2001-2003.

TN: Tom Nelson. Canadian, ex-army
27, male
Hair: blond
Weight: 15 St / 95.25 Kg
Height: 182cm
Race: Caucasian
Specific signs: tattooed
He has been twice accused of raping different women but was never convicted. He has worked on several oil rigs before Delta 12. No indication of any schooling.
Joined the army at 16, he has been sent to Afghanistan in 2002 and dismissed in 2006. He worked for Tar and Lot oil rigs before arriving on Delta 12.

GN: Geoff Nobst. U.S. ex-army
22, male

Hair: Black
Weight: 12 St / 78 Kg
Height: 177cm
Race: Caucasian
Specific signs: tattooed
A high school drop-out, he has joined the army soon after.

PR: Philippe Rowland, U.S. ex-marine
46, male
Hair: Black
Weight: 11 St / 70 Kg
Height: 180cm
Race: African American
Specific signs: tattooed
A veteran of the war in Afghanistan and Iraq; he has been
demobilized in 2005. He had many problems re-settling
into a normal civilian life.

AE: AL Ellys. British ex-army
39, male
Hair: Brown
Weight: 11.6 St / 74 Kg
Height: 168 Cm
Race: Caucasian
Specific signs: tattooed
He achieved 3 UK A levels (SATs and Achievement tests).
He has been posted in Germany until the late nineties,
went to Afghanistan in 2002 but didn't serve and was sent
back a few months later and worked on various oil rigs
ever since before joining Delta 12.

ED: Etienne Dutoit, French. Ex-army
26, male
Hair: Blond
Weight: 11.9 St / 76 Kg
Height: 6ft1
Race: Caucasian

Specific signs: tattooed
Grew up in a village where the sound of the church bells was so deafening that the actual sound has been embedded in his brain. Even now on Delta 12 the clocks are blasting at 8 am, Noon, 5 pm and 10 pm every day except Sunday at 9 am, 10 am, Noon, 7 pm, 8 pm and 9 pm. Banging incessantly and mercilessly, the sound of the church bells has been programmed inside him. It always chimes on the dot, inside his head.

The Medical Officer
Each month a new member of staff is appointed amongst the workers.

The Investigators

John Pediot, 38, American
Degree in Social Science, he spent four years working for the CIA, six years as head of investigation at Universal Insurance.

Jacqueline Smith, 29, English
Degree in Computer Sciences, six years as an investigator at Lloyds insurance, four years as a special investigator at the UK VAT Complex Unit.

Jeremy Vine, 55, American
Ex Lieutenant NYPD and spent five years as head investigator at the IRS.

Jack Wilcox, 56, English
PhD in Investigating Psychology, two years assigned to Chicago Police Welfare Unit, four years working with ex-military combatants returning from the war front.

Character description
The special investigating team known as **JJJJ**, named after the first initial of their first name are often assembled and called in to examine large and complex international cases. The team is surprisingly well disciplined and trained. Fit, vigilant, cunning and extremely meticulous, health conscious and non-smokers.

The team can spend hours arguing, debating and researching.

One Main Narrator

Six military officers inside a military base in Austin, Texas

Sets

1. **Delta 12, oil rig**

2. **The White Room (The Investigating Room)**

Around a table
Four investigators have 24 hours to solve the whole
investigation. Each and one of them present their views
and findings.
Within 24 hours they will debate, argue, demonstrate and
unwind a treasure trove of information that each
investigator gathered over a period of three months prior
to the meeting.

The White Room
The whole story emerges from the White Room.
There is a large empty space, about 6000 sq feet by 6000,
only filled with a large oblong metallic table furnished
with four comfortable armchairs. The furniture is new and
fairly contemporary. The four leather-bound armchairs
seem to match the surface of the table, which is white.

The ceiling is very high. Six rows of neon lights stand
sentinel above the room. The walls are all bright white;
freshly painted. No windows. The examination room is

located in a basement. Several air flow fans are located in each corner of the ceiling. There is an omnipresent smell of fresh paint in the room. The room is fairly warm. There are several radiators on the walls.

Jars of fresh water and glasses are on the table with flasks of hot coffee with cold milk along with a choice of sugar and biscuits. The table is soon filled with the appropriate files, paperwork and laptops.

3. At a military base

Set in an office inside a military base in Austin, Texas. Six military officers are present with NP (scene 11).

Glossary

Ground Control is based in Austin, Texas, USA at the offices of The Sun's Corporation.

One of the pirates' boats boarded Delta 12 by the A-deck and another one on the B-Deck soon afterwards.
Hands free microphone enable a recording of events then the sound file is emailed as a log.

Logs are text, images and sound files.

The Sun Industries is an oil and commodities business and the lease holder of the Delta 12 oil rig platform.

Delta 12

A-Deck

COMM, level 1.

Living quarters
Infirmary
Storage 1
Storage 2
Dorm 2
Storage 2
Bath 2
Play Room / Gym

B-Deck

Energy room
Water tank reserve
Dorm 1
Bath 1
Kitchen, level 2
Heating room
Water
Oil tanks, level 1

Upper A-Deck

Helipad
Bridge for sea boarding
Bridge into B-Deck

Upper B-deck

Bridge for sea boarding
Bridge into A-Deck

Music and background sound

Along with the sound of the ocean and the shrieking seagulls that are omnipresent, there is a deep and

distinctive sound of thunderstorms brewing all the way throughout when the story is in and around Delta 12. The sound of thunderstorms appears progressively and in crescendo like an on-going melody.

There is always a specific sound associated with each worker. The most relevant one is the sound of the church bells chiming inside ET's head.

Screenplay

Scene One: "In the White Room"

Narrator
Four high level investigators have been summoned in New York to investigate an insurance claim relating to the accidental death of six workers located off shore on an oil rig in the Atlantic Ocean for a total sum of $380, 000.000.

Displayed on the screen
The Investigators

John Pediot, 38, American
He has a degree in Social Science. He spent four years working for the CIA, six years as head of investigation at Universal Insurance.

Jacqueline Smith, 29, English
Degree in Computer Sciences, six years as an investigator at Lloyds insurance, four years as a special investigator at the UK VAT complex unit

Jeremy Vine, 55, American
Ex Lieutenant NYPD and has spent five years as a head investigator at the IRS.

Jack Wilcox, 56, English

PhD in Investigating Psychology, two years assigned to
Chicago Police Welfare Unit, four years working with ex-
military combatants returning from the War front.
The special investigating team known as **JJJJ**, named after
the first initial of their names are often assembled and
called in to examine large and complex international cases.
The team is surprisingly well disciplined and trained. Fit,
vigilant, cunning and extremely meticulous, health
conscious and non-smokers.

Jacqueline Smith

Gentleman… We have twenty-four hours to investigate
this claim. We may break at any time, individually for
short breaks, then return. Please leave all the notes and
documents on the table. It is safe; there will always be one
of us in here. Please be seated.

*The investigators are removing their coats, sit, and adjust
their swivel armchairs.*

Jacqueline Smith

Staring at a clock displayed on her laptop monitor
And the time begins right now!

Scene Two: "Delta 12"

View of Delta 12
Opening credits and title

The list of the staff members and situation is displayed on the screen.

Narrator

Current situation:
Present team arrived on the first of January 2007 on Delta 12.

In the White Room
Jack Wilcox reads the list of the staff and the comments about each member of the staff is read by John Piedot.

Jack Wilcox

Staff

AP: Allan Patterson. U.S. ex-army
26, male

Hair: Black
Weight: 12 St / 82 kg
Height: 6ft 4
Race: Caucasian
Specific signs: tattooed

John Pediot

He contracted a heroin addiction whilst at sea. When the dependence is too severe the doctor in charge always prescribes some pills of some kind to ease the need and release the tension. In the U.S. army the use of heavy drugs is a very sensitive and controversial subject. Officially, there is none but when at war and programmed to kill there is little less that can help.

No one really knows what the tablets contain. It tastes and feels like aspirin but works a treat. It seriously brings the tension down.

Jack Wilcox

DC: Don Carradine. U.S. ex-army
22, male
Hair: Brown
Weight: 11 St / 75 Kg
Height: 5.11
Race: Caucasian
Specific signs: tattooed

John Pediot

No schooling known. It is believed that he was enrolled into the army in 2003. He worked for six months on an oil rig prior to Delta 12. It was his first oil job. He was further distinguished the by a perpetual blinking of the eyes, and this, together with the red tint of his complexion and a way he had of hanging his head forward and rolling it from side to side when he walks, gave him the appearance of an orangutan.

Jack Wilcox

DNC: Dabiel N. Caldley. U.S. ex-army
38, male
Hair: Cropped/Grey
Weight: 12 St / 82 Kg
Height: 5ft 8"
Race: Caucasian
Specific signs: tattooed

John Pediot

A High school dropout, he joined the army soon after and went to war in Afghanistan in 2001-2003.

Jack Wilcox

NP: Nathan Pearl. U.S. ex-marine
44, male
Hair: Red
Weight: 11 St / 75 Kg
Height: 6ft
Race: Caucasian
Specific signs: tattooed

John Pediot

A High school dropout, he has joined the army soon after. He joined the war in Afghanistan in 2001-2003.

Jack Wilcox

TN: Tom Nelson. Canadian, ex-army
27, male
Hair: blond
Weight: 15.0 St / 95.25 Kg
Height: 182cm
Race: Caucasian
Specific signs: tattooed

John Pediot

He has been twice accused of raping different women but
was never convicted. He has worked on several oil rigs
before Delta 12. No indication of any schooling.
Joined the army at 16, he has been sent to Afghanistan in
2002 and dismissed in 2006. He worked for Tar and Lot oil
rigs before arriving on Delta 12.

Jack Wilcox

GN: Geoff Nobst. U.S. ex-army
22, male
Hair: Black
Weight: 12 St / 78 Kg
Height: 177cm
Race: Caucasian
Specific signs: tattooed

John Pediot

A High-school dropout. Joined the army soon after.

Jack Wilcox

PR: Philippe Rowland, U.S. ex-marine
46, male
Hair: Black
Weight: 11 St / 70 Kg
Height: 180cm
Race: African American
Specific signs: tattooed

John Pediot

A veteran of the war in Afghanistan and Iraq, he has been demobilized in 2005. He had many problems re-settling into a normal civilian life.

Jack Wilcox

AE: Al Ellys. British ex-army
39, male
Hair: Brown
Weight: 11.6 St / 74 Kg
Height: 168 Cm
Race: Caucasian
Specific signs: tattooed

John Pediot

He is English/British. He achieved 3 UK A levels (SAT and Achievement tests). He has been posted in Germany until the late nineties, went to Afghanistan in 2002 but didn't serve and was sent back a few months later and worked on various oil rigs ever since before joining Delta 12.

Jack Wilcox

ED: Etienne Dutoit, French. Ex-army
26, male
Hair: Blond
Weight: 11.9 St / 76 Kg
Height: 6ft1
Race: Caucasian

Specific signs: tattooed

John Pediot

Grew up in a village where the sound of the church bells was so deafening that the sound has been embedded in his brain. Even now on Delta 12 the clocks are blasting at 8 am, Noon, 5 pm and 10 pm every day except Sunday at 9 am, 10 am, Noon, 7 pm, 8 pm, and 9 pm.

Banging incessantly and mercilessly, the sound of the church bells has been programmed inside him. It always chimes on the dot, inside his head.

Jeremy Vine

Reading the files

The Rules

There are no women on board. There is a captain and his eight soldiers, all heavily armed with hand-guns and rifles,

always on duty. Everyone is the captain, the soldier and the medical officer. There is a staff rotation in shifts.

Each crew member must compile a daily log of his life on the oil rig.

The Sun Industries Corp trades in oil and commodities and is the owner of the Delta 12 oil rig platform. The company is based in Austin, Texas.

Smoking is not allowed anywhere on the platform. Heroin is widely available albeit in moderation. It is unofficially smuggled with the food.

Officially the company doesn't provide any needles. It is however possible to inject heroin inside the infirmary. The needles are often dumped at sea. There are long periods of 2-3 weeks without heroin and it's when the tension mounts and fights occur amongst the crew.

Pills of some kind are provided as a substitute by the medical officer in charge. Officially no tablets or pills of any kind are being distributed.

No one really knows what the tablets contain. It tastes and feels like some aspirin but works a treat. It seriously brings the tension down.

A job at sea on an oil rig is one of the only jobs available for a serviceman where he does not have to kill. In order to

sustain the hardship endure at sea there is little to relieve the pressure.

Every month a new member of staff is appointed amongst the workers to become the medical officer.

The living quarters consist of a recreation room with TV sets, tables and sofas, a large canteen, a kitchen, a gym and the dorms: a large room with bunk beds.

There is very little heat and it's very cold, especially at night. The living conditions are extremely harsh, the food is lousy, the washrooms and the toilets although cleaned up every day, are constantly filthy, dirty water is always leaking over the floors.

There is no escape possible for the duration of the contract, which generally lasts for one year. A worker may only leave on serious medical grounds or if dead. Death and suicides are a common occurrence.

No cigarettes or drugs are allowed on the platform. Anyone found to contravene the rules will be sent to a cell with no light and no window for twenty-four or forty-eight hours depending on the crime.

A medical doctor comes in every three months to inspect the men and distribute medicines. No one would ever admit to any serious illness or disease as this would be interpreted as a sign of weakness. Any admission of weakness to fellow workers will drive anyone to suicide.

Every now and then a man escapes by plunging into the sea. No one has ever survived an escape as the sea is infested with sharks.

Mutiny is rare and when there is one the captain can order one of his soldiers to shoot or if it gets really serious the captain can send a message to the Nigerian coast guards and the army generally arrive in a jiffy.

Sometimes, an army ship Nigerian or American is seen on the horizon.

The weather is always lousy and the sea always stormy. The work is extremely demanding, channeling the dig of oil for eight hours, one hour for lunch and some occasional breaks. The workers start their day at 5 am and the curfew, when all lights are switched off, at 10 pm.

Every week an oil cargo arrives to take a load of oil.

Sometimes there is an attack from some sea pirates. They board the oil platform; take members of the crew hostage often with accomplices amongst the crew. Sometimes the pirates escape with their load of oil but most of the time the army is called in and it's when the carnage starts. It always leads to the death of some of the hostages.

The pirates who are captured are taken to the main land and are always hanged in Nigeria without trial.

This is the life on an oil platform off the coast of Africa, one of the most violent places on earth.

The average salary is $4000 a month, plus living expenses. In spite of all this, there will always be someone willing to join a crew of the men on the many oil platforms.

Each man is reporting on everyone's daily life; each and one of them reports on everyone. It is a constant surveillance. Each and one of them are the head and the keeper of the other. Everyone is watching one another.

Everyone must keep a log of the events that will be emailed to The Sun's central office (their employer Austin Texas, USA). –Also nick-named: "Ground Control". Everyone is in charge or everyone believes it is so.

Scene 3: "History of the country"

John Pediot gets up suddenly and leaves the room.

Jack Wilcox

Reading a file
Nigeria is the world's sixth largest exporter of crude oil, holds the fourth largest reserve of oil and gas and is an important supplier of oil to the U.S. Since the British left

Nigeria in the 1960s the country has been in a state of semi-civil war, wracked by religious conflicts, and its natural resources looted by western companies, as a result of which millions of people have died.

The country earns 75 per cent of its revenue from oil and in 2004 had foreign debts of $33bn. Although repayment of the debt is slowly improving production may also be held back by deteriorating social conditions in the oil producing Niger Delta.

While the average number of different ethnic nationalities in each African country is about 46, Nigeria comprises about 250, many of whom did not even know of the existence of the other before merging.

Not even the colonial government knew the exact number of tribes and languages. Nigeria underwent the period of colonization from 1865 to 1960.

Scene Four: "Life on the oil rig"

The White Room

All investigators are in the room.

Jacqueline Smith

1. What does it transpire?

Jeremy Vine

I'm sorry?

Jacqueline Smith

2. How long each man has been living in such condition?

Jack Wilcox

3. Condition? You mean working on the rig?

Jacqueline Smith

4. Don't they ever get a Lady in there?

John Pediot

-Only a fearless female soldier or a butch dyke can endure such an environment.

Jack Wilcox

-You're talking male chimps there...Animals!

Jacqueline Smith
5. I thought they were male soldiers?

Jack Wilcox
-You know damn well what I mean...

Jacqueline Smith
-I suppose…

Jacqueline Smith
6. The question was: how long each man has been living on Delta 12? Was it the first time?

John Pediot
Reading through the list of workers

Jeremy Vine
7. It is like inside a jail…

John Pediot
-No it's not!

Jack Wilcox
- Hell it is!

Jacqueline Smith
-Hell it is!

Jack Wilcox

8. Jail is where ... one is deprived of freedom of movements, of choices and above all the ability to survive without female... force, pay other men to submit to their needs. In jail, it's not a job. They do not get paid. On the oil rig there is no imprisonment. It's a voluntary condition.

John Pediot

-Voluntary, they need the money but it's still voluntary.

Jeremy Vine

-There's no evidence of forced sex between the workers. It's unthinkable. A worker can easily report this or sue or get help. Besides, all workers are soldiers of an equal and opposite force. They are all tough animals.

Jack Wilcox

-And it's complete isolation.

Jeremy Vine

-One might help himself...

Jack Wilcox

-As one does...
Laughter from Jack Wilcox and Jeremy Vine

Jacqueline Smith

-Can we return to the investigation please?

John Pediot

-Yes. So, it's a near complete isolation type of environment. Complete celibacy. Like inside a monastery, albeit a violent one. A willingness to brave the harshest and otherwise unbearable conditions to earn money…

Jack Wilcox

-and to satisfy a need…

Jacqueline Smith

-Isn't a soldier's prerogative?

Jeremy Vine

-What is?

Jacqueline Smith

-Violence?

John Pediot

-A soldier's prerogative is to kill!

Jacqueline Smith

9. What do they do in their spare time?
What do they think about?
What do they talk about?

John Pediot

-They do not think and they do not talk! They work, they eat, they sleep and they fight between themselves. That's their job. That's their life!

Jacqueline Smith

-Why are some of the logs handwritten? Can't they type?

John Pediot

-Some do. A lot of logs are manually generated or the staff can record their own voice describing their log.

Scene Five: "Preparing the investigation"

Jeremy Vine is reading through some notes. Jack Wilcox and John Piedot are absent.

Jeremy Vine

Reading and muttering words aloud whilst Jacqueline Smith is arranging the files

22 logs: AP TO BASE
END DC
TN TO BASE: END TN
AE TO BASE: END AE

Scene 6: "Country File"

In the White Room, all investigators are present.

Jack Wilcox

Reading a file
Nigeria was granted full independence from the British

Empire in 1960, as a federation of three regions (Northern, Western, Eastern), each retaining a substantial measure of self-government.

In 1966, two successive coups by different groups of army officers brought the country under military rule. The leaders of the second coup tried to increase the power of the federal government and replaced the regional governments with twelve state governments.

The constant disruption in the oil production and the state of semi-civil war with the locals started to bear a huge impact on the revenues of the main operators in the region Tar, Lot and Sure.

The Nigerian government is now responding with a different approach and is also answering to the growing criticism from the international community.

Over 200 000 people have died so far in religious conflicts. The country has been unstable for all of its forty years since independence.

All the institutions established by the colonial government have been destroyed beyond recognition.

They include the public services, the educational system, the judiciary, and the legal system, the railways, electricity supply and water.

The country counts nearly 200 million inhabitants divided into 36 states with very little in common.

The region has suffered from immense pollution and total lack of infrastructure ever since the first company started to dig oil in 1958. Output is frequently disrupted by the activities of the local tribes and criminal gangs are frequently destroying the oil infrastructure. In 2003 a number of gangs kidnapped oil workers and their families.

The response is always swift and ferocious, it's the army who always reply to the provocation and destroy the tribes' villages.

Scene 7: "Job description 1"
In the White Room, John Piedot and Jacqueline Smith have left the room.

Jack Wilcox
Reading a file.
A series of highly disturbing and intriguing images of oil exploration is being presented.

Workers performing hot work such as welding, cutting, brazing, soldering, and grinding are exposed to the risk of fires from ignition of flammable or combustible materials in the space, and from leaks of flammable gas into the space, from hot work equipment.

Potential Hazard:
Getting burned by fires or explosions during hot work.

Possible Solutions:
The basic precautions for fire prevention are:
Perform hot work in a safe location, or with fire hazards removed or covered.

Special Precautions:

Do not perform hot work where flammable vapors or combustible materials exist. Work and equipment should be relocated outside of the hazardous areas, when possible. Make suitable fire-extinguishing equipment immediately available. Such equipment may consist of pails of water, buckets of sand, hose, or portable extinguishers.

Assign additional personnel (fire watch) to guard against fire while hot work is being performed. Fire watchers are required whenever welding or cutting is performed in locations where anything greater than a minor fire might develop.

Fire watchers shall:
Have fire-extinguishing equipment readily available and be trained in its use.

Be familiar with facilities for sounding an alarm in the event of a fire.

Watch for fires in all exposed areas and to extinguish them. Maintain the fire watch at least half hour after completion of welding or cutting operations to detect and extinguish possible smoldering fires.

Potential Hazard:
Getting burned by a flash fire or explosion that results from an accumulation of flammable gases such as Methane or Hydrogen around the wellhead area:

Possible Solutions:

Monitor the atmosphere with a gas detector. If a flammable or combustible gas exceeds 10 per cent of the lower explosive level (LEL), the work must be stopped.

Identify the source of the gas and repair the leakage.
Well Control

If the well doesn't produce adequately, a beam pumping unit may be installed.

There are four basic types of beam pumping units. Three involve a walking beam to power the pump. The fourth reciprocates by winding a cable on and off a rotating drum. The job of all four types is to change the circular motion of an engine to the reciprocating motion of the pump.

The pump units are brought in disassembled on ships and off-loaded onsite. The many parts of the pump unit include large heavy metal pieces that need to be assembled.

Scene 8: "The Job"

In the White Room. All the investigators are present.
John Pediot is reading a file.

John Pediot

Well Completion
Once the design well depth is reached, the formation must be tested and evaluated to determine whether the well will be completed for production, or plugged and abandoned.

To complete the well production, casing is installed and cemented and the drilling rig is dismantled and moved to the next site.

Daily drilling report n: a record made each day of the operations on a working drilling rig and, traditionally, phoned, faxed, emailed, or radioed to The Sun every morning.

derrick n: a large load-bearing structure, usually of bolted construction. In drilling, the standard derrick has four legs standing at the corners of the substructure and reaching to the crown block. The substructure is an assembly of heavy beams used to elevate the derrick and provide space to install blowout preventers, casing heads, and so forth.

derrick floor n: also called the rig floor.

Derrick hand n: the crew member who handles the upper end of the drill string as it is being hoisted out of or lowered into the hole. On a drilling rig, he or she may be responsible for the circulating machinery and the conditioning of the drilling or work over fluid.

Cement Job...
Jeremy Vine interrupts.

Jeremy Vine
I think we're getting the picture.

Jacqueline Smith
Besides, most of the digging has been done before this team arrived. The team is only there to take the oil, load the oil on the ships and guard the rig.

Jack Wilcox
The surrounding is already tough enough. The main tasks are just a factory job.

Scene 9: "Job description 2"

In the White Room, all inspectors are present.
Jeremy Vine is reading PR's log. It's an email received from Ground Control.

Jeremy Vine

As the work has become far too demanding we need new workers. Here is the list of Job Responsibilities.

You will provide practical, functional leadership to a team of safety representatives and field-based safety leaders, undertaking practical safety training, and will use your detailed sector and technical knowledge to support the Group and Regional safety team in improving the Safety Management System (SMS) and delivering the annual safety plan. You will be well-versed in working effectively within a team.

You will have proven on-shore and off-shore experience. Job Description: Offshore Pipeline Project Engineer – 2-3 years of experience. Degree qualified, preferable in civil or mechanical engineering. Must be able to communicate clearly and write professional reports and must be able to operate independently or to supervise others. An understanding of the following other disciplines would also be useful: mechanical equipment / structural design / process/ electrical / instrumentation / control systems/ health and safety/ risk analysis.

John Piedot
Pouring some coffee in his cup
I'm sorry to interrupt but is there any Soy milk around?

Jacqueline Smith

No. Cow's milk only!

Jeremy Vine

Ahem... Main Duties: take full technical responsibility for the execution of work in specified project and technology areas; direct the work of small teams of staff within a larger project or direct small project teams; identify the objectives for the project team assigned by the Project Manager and communicate these to team members working in the same area.

Jacqueline Smith

It's indeed an impressive job description. It's a pity that none of the workers do fit the profile. Apart from a stint in the army, most of them haven't even completed their schooling or college years.

Scene 10 "Analysis"

In the White Room only Jacqueline Smith and Jeremy Vine are present.

Jeremy Vine reads a private email from PR.

Jeremy Vine
The way I see it there is very little difference between America and Africa. It can be just as sizzling hot. It can be cold too. Really, really cold off the coast of Africa. When the sun shines and its power is felt far beneath our entrails; it's like a shot of heroin or a slit from a knife in your veins. You feel it deep.
Jack Wilcox grabs a log. The voice of TN is heard over a series of images.

TN
TN Log 6532
Today there was a major fight between GN, PR and AE. It started on an argument over some lost powder. GN thought PR took it. AE lost one tooth in the fight and PR and GN were severely bruised. AE's face is now green and blue. They have all refused to get examined by me. I was the duty medical this month. The toilet floor and one of the sinks were recovered with blood. It was a major blood bath. I didn't know three men could have leaked that much blood.

Scene 11 "The Situation"

In the White Room, everyone is present.
John Piedot looks at another log. DC's voice is heard over a series of images displayed on the screen and passed over between the investigators during the reading.

DC

DC Log 8124
6 AM. I'm stuck in the Comm. I heard a roaring noise coming from several gun shots. I heard people screaming. There was a loud pounding noise. I just knew straight away what happened. We have been boarded. I quickly fired an SOS to Ground Control. I heard more gun shots and the sound of scuttling then what followed I guessed was some heavy fighting. I quickly locked myself inside the cabin.

There was a loud shrieking cry. Either someone was being tortured to death or someone was involved in a heavy accident. I fired another SOS as I still didn't get a response from the first one; strange! Ground Control is supposed to be very prompt to respond in a case like this.

Over to the investigators

Jacqueline Smith
Stop! Freeze there! Why is Ground Control supposed to respond promptly?

Jeremy Vine

Why is Ground Control waiting for a few minutes before responding?

All the investigators are taking notes. The camera is on the face of the investigators. The anguish is clearly seen over the investigators' face.

Back to DC's log

DC

I didn't want to use the radio to send a Mayday to draw any attention. To avoid making any noises. I just knew what went on. Some pirates boarded the rig. It happens. It has never happened with the current team. I was agonizingly holding my breath and pissing myself.

I couldn't go out. I couldn't breathe. I was stranded. Empty handed.

Another long agonizing moment and I heard further gun shots. Then the roaring noise I first heard started again. I heard people shouting, running then screaming, in that order. My heart was pounding inside my chest.
The roaring noise faded away gradually. I went back to the logs. It was another ten minutes of excruciating hell. This time apart from the noise of the shrieking seagulls, it was quiet in comparison.

My mail has now been answered.
"MESSAGE FROM GROUND CONTROL

Received your Maydays. Army patrol on the way. Stay put. Don't move."

Back to DC's LOG

DC

I peed in my trousers again.
Released a deep breath
I was all sweating from all over the place.
"Don't move! Stay Put" I can't move! I'm frozen man!
I just received another mail from Ground Control.

"MESSAGE FROM GROUND CONTROL
Army Patrol apprehended the pirates. All under control.
Nothing more to report for now. Keep your logs flowing!"

Real time audio recording

What happened on the rig? What happened? It's all quiet now. I feel suddenly very alone. Empty. Fuck! I decide to leave the room.

Scene 12: "The Massacre"

NP's description of the massacre.

A few days later after the boarding: an interview of NP with the military investigators. Set inside a military base, near the Sun Corporation offices in Austin, Texas.

NP is sitting at a table facing six military officers.

NP's description of the event:

NP

It must have been 8 AM. We were all on B-Deck where we normally go early in the morning.

We spend months without seeing anyone so if anyone would come; we either take notice straight away or don't even see anyone. There is a sense of abstraction going on here. It's like seeing a mirage if indeed we can see it. We

can't believe it is real until it hits us in the face. I guess that's what isolation does to some people.

We first saw the pirates boarding through A-Deck and stupidly we rushed to see them and stop them. We weren't armed. The element of surprise caught us right into it.

Then a few minutes later another set of pirates boarded from B-Deck. We walked in fact right into their trap. We were done for. They were all armed with guns, knives and Ks. They were all masked; all African and about thirty of them.

A few of them ordered us to sit down, telling us that we are being held as hostages. As we were about to sit down, a dispute emerged between a few of them. They started arguing, they shouted, one fired some shots in the air. I'm not sure what exactly happened after that. One of us panicked and tried to take the knife of a pirate. Then everyone panicked, everyone was screaming and the pirates started shooting indiscriminately at everyone, including some of the pirates. I've been shot a few times in my left arm and in my chest then lost consciousness. The next thing I knew was hearing DC's voice shouting my name. I think until today, I did not fully comprehend what exactly happened. It happened fast, very fast.

Scene 13: "The Tableau of the Massacre"

DC audio file

DC

With the hands-free microphone
I'm opening the door to the A-Deck.

Pause. About one minute. View of the A-Deck

I can barely believe my eyes. The stench is unbearable. I'm
not sure what the smell is. I'm walking on the deck.

Oh. Jesus. It's... it's, it's... The body of Jay and Ted and...
Fuck...
I stumble over a pool of blood.
The A-Deck is red, bloody red.
The sea is storming in the back and a flock of seagulls and
other ugly birds are gathering pace around Delta 12.
Bloody vultures!
I can see AP. He's dead too. His face has been... Oh God...
ripped opened with a knife, I guess.
ED is riddled with gun wounds. He has been shot several
times; in the heart and in the head and no... In the back of
the head too...
He didn't have time to shut his eyes.
Swallowing
Aaaaa...
He places his hand over ED's face and closes his eyes

I move my left hand towards his face and close his eyes.

I move toward a group of four bodies; four Africans, four pirates; all shot dead.

Vomiting

Rhhhhh...

Gasping. Exhaling

Where are the others?

I cross over the bridge to B-Deck.

It's, it's... there are about nine people lying on the deck. Dead pirates and the fucking seagulls... Someone... Someone seem to be moving. Yes, he is trying to move... blood over his face. I can't see who...

He screams

NP? TN? The face has been carved with a knife. It's NP! He is alive and yes, yes TN is also there, he's moving too. God, god...

I'm trying to carry NP first. I take him to the infirmary on A-Deck level.

NP! NP it's DC. Can you hear me? Can you hear me? Speak man, speak for fuck's sake!

He moves his left hand.

We are approaching the infirmary.

Heavy breathing

I place NP on one of the two beds. I pour some water over his wounds then some antiseptic. He is moving. He's uttering some grunting sound. Hell! He is alive. NP... I need to fetch TN. I will be back. Stay put!

I leave him there and I'm running back over B-deck to fetch TN.

Running over B-Deck

Fucking seagulls everywhere! The noise... The noise is deafening. Bloody beasts! Get out!
Pushing and beating the seagulls away
The seagulls are attacking TN
Fuck sake. TN. TN I'm here. I drag TN through hell. Hell, it is. Fuck. Thousands of birds around; it stinks and the noise... On A-Deck now entering level 1; I'm taking TN to the infirmary. There we are.
I place TN on the other bed. TN, speak to me for fuck's sake... Move!
Noises of gun shots can be heard
I hear some gun shots on the deck. I open the door. It's the U.S. navy patrol shooting at the birds. Fuck.
Falling on the floor
Fuck. I fell. The army is clearing the bodies and the men are taking them to their ship.
Agonizing on the floor
Help! Help! Two are inside the infirmary! Help...
Two marines are lifting me up. I can see that some marines are carrying NP and TN. They are taking them to their ship. A helicopter is landing on A-Deck and the guys are taking me inside. I'm the last member of the crew to leave Delta 12.

End of Broadcast.

Scene 14: "TN log".

In the White Room
Jack Wilcox is reading some notes.

Jack Wilcox

TN's log is not available. TN had some severe concussions in the head and is currently suffering from amnesia. He is still being treated.

Scene 15: "The Claim"

Jacqueline Smith and Jeremy Vine are waiting patiently for John Pediot and Jack Wilcox to return. After nearly one minute of intense and agonizing wait John Pediot returns all in sweat; he apologizes for being late.

John Pediot

Sorry for the wait...

He wipes his face with a tissue taken from the table, pours himself a glass of water and drinks it.

A few seconds later Jack Wilcox returns to the White Room. He stands for a few seconds behind his chair with an austere and demure look on his face. He then coughs

without paying too much attention to the other inspectors. Everyone is getting increasingly impatient.

John Pediot, a biscuit in his mouth burps loudly enough to finally catch the attention of the rest of the room. Jeremy Vine smiles, Jack Wilcox tries to ignore it and Jacqueline is getting very agitated.

Jacqueline shakes her head disapprovingly and coughs a bit with a tissue over her mouth and tries to re-shape her hairstyle... whilst all this is taking place Jeremy Vine is trying to sort out the mess they have made with the files over the desk.

John Pediot reads the claim

John Pediot

Memos 33332
Summary of the Claim

Claim for: Accidental Death
Group claim: Yes
Individual Claim: No
Quantity: 6
Capacity: Staff worker
Place: Oil Rig- Delta 12 Miles Latitude Atlantic Ocean

Names: AP Allan Patterson, DC Don Carradine, DNC Daniel N. Caldley, NP Nathan Pearl, TN Tom Nelson, GN

Geoff Nobst, PR Philippe Rowland, AE AL Ellys, ED Etienne Dutoit.

Validation: Insurance from the beginning of employment First of January 2007 until First of January 2008. [One year] Initiated by: The Sun Corporation based in Austin, Texas USA

Total amount: $380, 000.000
Premium: Paid
Payment: One off yearly 1.5 M
Status: Valid
Type of Insurance: Bundle; Accident, Liability, death, medical.

After reading the details of the coverage, the debate over the claim is very lively. Everyone is getting agitated, often cutting anyone in mid-sentence whilst everyone carries on with the debate, replying in crescendo mode.

Jacqueline Smith

So, it's not an accident

Jack Wilcox

An "Act of God"!

Jacqueline Smith

An "Act of God"? A rampage! A carnage!

John Pediot

Man-made carnage...

Jeremy Vine

An accidental carnage

Jack Wilcox

An accidental carnage as an "Act of God"

Jacqueline Smith

It's not an "Act of God"! It's a human massacre

Jeremy Vine

It's an accident

Jacqueline Smith

The oil rig has been boarded by some pirates in a violent...

John Pediot

...But the pirates have been intercepted

Jacqueline Smith

...and this resulted in an ugly, bloody bath...

Jack Wilcox

...the perpetrators have been caught and...

Jeremy Vine

...Six workers died and...

John Pediot

...it happens, it's an accident that...

Jacqueline Smith

...An accident waiting to happen...

Jeremy Vine

...waiting to happen?

Jack Wilcox

Nigeria is run by dictators and the country is overfilled by rebels, terrorists and poverty. This results in a constant fight to re-appropriate the resources and that includes the oil.

John Pediot

The oil company operates legitimately!

Jack Wilcox

They have a license. They pay their dues to exploit the oil and receive the protection by the Nigerian military that they are paying for.

Jacqueline Smith

Yes, but the country has never really been democratized. It's riddled by corruption. It's the most fraudulent country in the world and...

Jeremy Vine

...and the most violent

Jack Wilcox

Right, and...

Jacqueline Smith

...And out of nearly 200 million inhabitants -the most populous country in Africa- about 90% live in abject poverty and in constant war with their own government.

John Pediot

It's an accidental death waiting to happen...

Jeremy Vine

But that's neither here nor there. The company must have known that they are digging that oil in such a hostile environment and...

Jack Wilcox

...but both the insurance company and re-insurer must have known about this...

John Pediot

...that's why the premium is so big.

Jack Wilcox

Not that big: $1.5 M!

Jacqueline Smith

What's the price on human life?

Jack Wilcox

The oil company is doing a job, the government is doing their job in providing the licenses and the insurance company and the re-insurer are doing their job by insuring the oil rig and the workers.

John Pediot

And the workers are doing their job of...

Jacqueline Smith

...being killed and...

Jack Wilcox

...that's the job on an oil rig off the coast of Africa.

Jeremy Vine

If the state of the country was so well known, why would an insurance company even agree to insure and why for such a small premium?

John Pediot

... $1.5 M. of premium for all the workers isn't much

Jack Wilcox

Anything can happen on an oil rig; anywhere in the world and not only in Africa. History is full of deadly accidents on an oil rig.

John Pediot

Not full of it and accidents due to human errors mainly or poor maintenance...

Jeremy Vine

...Right. Not in war-like circumstances...

Jack Wilcox

...inside a country; in a state of semi-civil war...

John Pediot

...Correction. It's not inside a state or a country; it's off-shore!

Jeremy Vine

What does the "Memo" say?

Jacqueline Smith

Reading
.... Latitude...

Jack Wilcox

Eating a biscuit
Was the exact location mentioned in the original insurance form?

Jacqueline Smith is shuffling through the documents

Jeremy Vine
Stands up and helps finding the right memo. Short pause
Got it!

Reading
… From Latitude… *Whispering Short pause*
...Location...

Jacqueline Smith
Was the word "Africa" even mentioned?

John Pediot
And "Nigeria"?

Jeremy Vine
No. No mention: only the latitude inside the Atlantic
Ocean.

Jacqueline Smith
For what the insurer knew it could have been in the
middle of the Atlantic...

Jack Wilcox
The Atlantic is one of the deepest digs amongst all the
oceans...

John Pediot
…Not as deep as inside the Pacific!

Jeremy Vine
It may be harder to dig oil there but there are not any known pirates roaming inside the Atlantic Ocean...

Jacqueline Smith
...No, but there is off the coast of Nigeria!

John Pediot
One of the most violent and most populated countries in the world...

Jack Wilcox
...A country that has almost lived its entire history -since the departure of the British troops in the Sixties- in a state of semi-civil war.

Jeremy Vine
How can both the insurer and re-insurer could have been so duped in this way?

John Pediot
For them it was in the Atlantic Ocean somewhere...

Jacqueline Smith
Can't they calculate the latitude?

Jeremy Vine
Not many can...

Jack Wilcox

… It's an oversight…

John Pediot

We're talking major oversight here!

Jeremy Vine

Yep

Jacqueline Smith

The biggest oversight was for the oil company and the workers…

Jack Wilcox

How do you mean?

Jacqueline Smith

Well, for the oil company to knowingly employ workers with a likely chance to be massacred and for the staff to be totally ignorant of the situation.

Jeremy Vine

The workers are soldiers. They only obey orders.

John Pediot

…Trusting their employer!

Jack Wilcox

That's their prerogative and their job!

Jeremy Vine

Back to the claim: are we saying here that the insurance company has been misled?

Jacqueline Smith

They have been stupid. It's their fault for not calculating the latitude...

John Pediot

...Location is everything...

Jeremy Vine

...Latitudes...

Jacqueline Smith

...Indeed!

Small pause
The team is exhausted. They look around the room, at the paperwork lying disorderly on the desk again. They look at the walls, the ceiling...

John Pediot breaks the silence

John Pediot

Is it accidental death?

Jack Wilcox

No, it isn't.

John Pediot

Is it an "Act of God"?

Jacqueline Smith

An "Act of God"?

John Pediot

An "Act of God" is...

Jack Wilcox

It's a massacre, a multiple murder case. Six workers have
been killed by the pirates.

Jeremy Vine

The killers should pay...

Jack Wilcox

...The pirates?

Jeremy Vine

Yes

Jack Wilcox

Where are they now?

Jacqueline Smith

They probably got tortured for a bit by the Nigerian army
and then shot, in that order.

Jeremy Vine

No trial?

Jack Wilcox

In Africa?

John Pediot

So the Nigerian government should pay?

Jacqueline Smith

They could never pay.

Jeremy Vine

Then it's the oil company who is guilty...

Jacqueline Smith

Guilty all right! The government is guilty. We're all guilty.

Jack Wilcox

We are guilty?

Jacqueline Smith

We all need cheap oil and desperately so. Someone's got to do the job. We need oil. We all do.

Jeremy Vine

At the end of the day the oil company still paid a hefty premium to insure their workers and the insurance company and the re-insurer agreed to provide the cover...

Jack Wilcox

A claim has been made for accidental death. I believe it is accidental death.

Jeremy Vine

I agree...

John Pediot

..I concur...

Jacqueline Smith

This is all too revolting...

Jack Wilcox

It may well be so but that's not our job to be revolted. We have been assembled here to investigate a claim and we just did this.

John Pediot

Since they have assembled all of us to investigate the claim, the insurance company must have had some suspicions.

Jack Wilcox

They sure did. But we have been assembled here at the re-insurer's request.

Jeremy Vine

It is Accidental Death due to an "Act of God". The responsibility for both the insurer and the re-insurer company is then diminished...

Jacqueline Smith

Diminished?

Jeremy Vine

In case of an "Act of God" they can only pay and in this case for the value of the insurance's cover for the families of the victims. They only pay a percentage of the actual cover.

Jacqueline Smith

How much?

Jeremy Vine

It varies from the terms and conditions. It could be up to 80% of the cover.

John Pediot

You mean they deduce 80% of the cover for each worker?

Jeremy Vine

Right!

Jack Wilcox

So, they only pay 20% of the original cover...

Jeremy Vine

Correct!

Jacqueline Smith

Bloody crooks! Insurers never pay.

Jack Wilcox

It's an "Act of God" ...

Jacqueline Smith

...It bloody isn't...

Jeremy Vine

Are we all in favor of Accidental death by an "Act of God"?

Jack Wilcox and John Pediot

Yes

Jeremy Vine

Looking at Jacqueline Smith

And You?

Jacqueline Smith

I do not seem to have much of a choice in this matter...
Looking at the clock from her laptop
...and our time is up!

Short pause.
Gentlemen... It has been an adventure...

Jack Wilcox

Yeah

Jeremy Vine

Thanks

John Pediot

Yep

Jacqueline Smith

Gentlemen, we have investigated the claim to the best of our abilities. We have moved closer than anyone would have to the truth of the affair. We've come closer to understand The Sun's vision and prerogatives.

They all stand up; getting their belongings together and re-file all the documents. They all leave the room one by one in an orderly fashion.

FADE TO BLACK
End credits